MW01519165

OUTER SPACE

: the region beyond the Earth's atmosphere
in which there are stars and planets

†

Editor-in-Chief: Christa Renee
Editor-in-Chief: Ami Komai
Editorial Assistant: Rikki Johnson
Designer: Eric Pfleeger
Art Director: Wesley Pfleeger

Publisher: Christa Renee & Ami Komai

Bright
Lite

Bright Lite Magazine
P.O. Box 93753
Los Angeles, CA 90093

brightlitemag.com

ISBN: 978-0-9977217-1-3
Library of Congress Control Number: 2016919606

Printed in Canada by The Prolific Group

CONTRIBUTORS

FRANCES AGUIRRE

JAMIE ALTOON

ALYSON ALIANO

AMELIA ARMSTRONG

TALYA AXEL

ERIN BATES

ASHA BAILEY

PIPER BINGHAM

SASHA BOGOSIAN

ELINOR BONIFANT

STELLA BONSTIN

LUCINDA BOYS

FLORA BREITBARD

AMANDA BURCH

EMERY CASUCCI

ELIZABETH COOK

ALEXANDRA COWARD

ANNAMARIE DAVIDSON

SAMI DRASIN

DEVLIN ELLA

ANGELA GOLEME

GEORGIA GOODMAN

LIZ GORALKA

DARCY HEMLEY

AVA PRESLEY HIGGINSON

CAMILLE JOFFE

JASMINE JOHNSON

JENNA JUST

CAROLYN KELLY

MEGHAN KERR

NOMI KUNTZ

CLAIRE LANCE

IZZY LANDRETH

LUCIA LENNOX

DANIELA MARTINEZ

AYDEN PELLE

AUBREY POEHLMAN

DOLLY PRATT

OLIVIA ROBINSON

FREYA RUSSELL

STELLA SINGER

SADIE JOULE SOM

ELLA VALENSI

ISABEL VIOLA

OLIVE WEIER

KHEFRI WILCOX

SERA WILCOX

KYLIE YOBE

SPECIAL CONTRIBUTORS

TODD CATHER

PAT DONMOYER

UAN CARLOS HERNÁNDEZ

MEGHAN KERR

TAM REID

JOHN THORNTON

CONTENTS

CONTENTS

Space Cat by Aubrey Poehlmann (age 10)

OUTER SPACE

Outer space is vast
Outer space is the unknown
Outer space is a mystery
Because all we know is home
Let's go!

IZZY LANDRETH AGE 11

A WORLD WITHOUT THE SUN

By Wesley Pfleeger, Age 10

Inside the
Jet Propulsion
Lab
Interview by Ami Komai

BL: What do you do at JPL*?

Sarah: I work for the Deep Space Network, or DSN, which is NASA's set of very large radio antennas (100-200 feet across!) that talk to interplanetary spacecraft. We have antennas in California, Spain, and Australia, and we support space missions from agencies around the world. My job is to help mission teams get their spacecraft ready to work with DSN, and to make sure DSN is ready to send the spacecraft data onward to the mission teams. Over the past few years, I've worked with mission teams studying the Sun, asteroids, Mercury, Mars, and Pluto.

BL: What made you want to work there?

S: A lot of companies and government agencies build spacecraft, but most of those stick around in Earth orbit. JPL is one of the few places in the world to work on missions going to other planets! At JPL, every spacecraft is unique, doing something new and adding to our knowledge of the universe.

BL: Did you always know you wanted to work in the space program, one way or another?

S: For a long time I thought I'd like to be an architect. I liked the idea of a job that combines math and creativity. Gradually during high school I came around to the idea of working in the space industry. At JPL, I've found plenty of opportunities to use math and creative problem solving, with the added benefit of turning science fiction into reality.

BL: What fascinates you most about space?

S: Like Star Trek says, space is "the final frontier." The incredible variety of celestial bodies out there – even just in our own solar system – means there's always something new to explore.

BL: What's the coolest thing thats happened to you working there?

S: It was amazing working with the New Horizons* mission last year when the spacecraft made its historic flyby of Pluto. During that time I got to see some of the latest and best images of Pluto ever taken up to that point, before they were even released to the public. It made me so proud to know that I had some small part in making sure those photos made it safely to Earth. I grew up with this vague idea that Pluto looks something like the moon, but now I know better! New Horizons is a mission managed by the Johns Hopkins Applied Physics Lab.*

BL: Sometimes technology developed as a solution to an outer space problem end up becoming useful here on earth too. Any inventions that our readers may not be aware of that originated either in the JPL or in the process of space exploration?

S: I don't know much about this, but I do know that a lot of technology developed for space ends up on Earth in applications like medical imaging. There are many examples like that.

BL: I imagine numbers and calculations being very important to the success of any project involving outer space. How does math play a role in your profession? Did you have to overcome any difficulties with math while a student or do you think the "math is hard" meme is a myth?

S: Math is very important at all stages of the engineering process, from the rough calculations to see if an idea is even possible, to the precision design specifications needed to build or navigate a spacecraft. My first job at JPL involved more math. In my current job, I don't do lots of detailed calculations, but I do need to understand enough to notice if the numbers are off. I'm constantly asking myself, "Does this make sense?" when looking at design specifications. Sometimes I do rough calculations in my head or on the computer. I've always been pretty comfortable with math, and I think it's fun. But I think I am "good at math" because I was taught how it can be fun, not the other way around. The more you practice it, the better you get, and you're more likely to practice something that's fun for you. I wonder if the idea that "math is hard" might actually come from a widespread feeling that "math is boring."

BL: What inspired you to get through all the years of schooling to get to where you are today?

S: In general, I liked being in school for its own sake, because I like learning. Sometimes, though, the day-to-day effort of classes and homework was hard work, or boring. I usually got through the hard times by imagining how the hard work now would make my life easier later.

BL: If you could visit anywhere in space (with a guaranteed safe return) where would you go?

S: I'd love to explore Titan, Saturn's largest moon. In some ways, Titan is a lot like Earth, only hundreds of degrees colder. Titan has an atmosphere, and it has lakes, clouds, and rain made out of methane. I would love to visit a place so similar to Earth and yet so alien at the same time.

BL: Are there any women in particular in the field of math and science that you look up to?

S: One woman I look up to in particular is Lindy Elkins-Tanton, a planetary scientist with whom I worked on an idea for a mission to a very cool asteroid called Psyche. I admire how Lindy has keen sense of curiosity, an incredible work ethic, and a way of bringing a team together – qualities that are very important in the field of space exploration, and that I want to improve in myself.

BL: Any advice for future astronauts, and young women fascinated with astronomy and space exploration?

S: Find the fun in what you choose to do. When you enjoy your work, you'll want to practice and get great at it.

photos by Darcy Hemley

*JPL:
The Jet Propulsion Laboratory (JPL) is a federally funded research and development center and NASA field center located in La Cañada Flintridge, California and Pasadena, California, United States. (wikipedia)

*John Hopkins Applied Physics Lab:
The Johns Hopkins University Applied Physics Laboratory (APL), located in Howard County, Maryland, near Laurel and Columbia, is a not-for-profit, university-affiliated research center employing 5,600 people. APL is primarily a defense contractor. It serves as a technical resource for the Department of Defense, NASA, and other government agencies. The Lab is an engineering research and development organization rather than an academic division of Johns Hopkins University.
(wikipedia)

Curiosity landed on Mars August 6, 2012 and it's two-year mission was extended indefinitely in December 2012.

It's mission is to investigate Martian climate and geology, assess if the chosen field site inside Gale Crater has ever offered environmental conditions favorable for microbial life, investigating presence of water, and whether the planet is habitable in preparation for future human exploration.

*New Horizons mission:
New Horizons is a NASA spacecraft that was the first to visit dwarf planet Pluto in July 2015. Its pictures of the dwarf planet's icy surface, as well as observations of Pluto's moon Charon, are revolutionizing our understanding of solar system objects far from the sun. (space.com)

SPACE

PLANTS

BY DEVLIN ELLA
AGE 13

MOONLESS NIGHT

BLOW A BIT OF STARDUST

INTO A MOONLESS NIGHT WATCH IT

SPARKLE AND TWINKLE

SEE THE BIRDS DANCE IN THE LIGHT

THE DARK CLOUDS DRIFT OFF

THE WINDS

TURN TO BREEZES

WATCH THE GLITTERING STARS

SEE AS EACH WINKS AND TEASES

CAMILLE JOFFE   AGE 12
LOS ANGELES

Ask Devlin
Age 13

BL: What is your bedtime routine and how long does it take?

Devlin: My bedtime routine has been basically the same since I was a wee sprout - bath, book, and bed. But now it has morphed into shower, read social media and bed.

BL: How do you find quiet time in a house with siblings?

Devlin: I do find it hard to find quiet time in our small house, where I share a room with my brother and sister. But usually I just go into our room, shut the door, and put in headphones. My siblings are usually in our playroom anyways. Sometimes my sister comes into the room and I just ask if I can have some quiet time and she usually leaves. Overall, my siblings and I all try to be respectful of each other and give each other space when we can.

BL: How do you deal with it when your parents won't let you do things your friends are doing?

Devlin: I have a very good group of friends, who usually don't do anything too outrageous. My parents trust me because I have earned that trust. I can't recall anything my parents haven't let me do that my friends have done. Plus, I feel close with my parents. So if it's important to me, they always allow me to plead my case.

BL: Have you ever gotten homesick at a sleepover or at camp? What did you do?

Devlin: When I was younger, I would get homesick at sleepovers all the time. But what helped me not get homesick was by going to shorter Girl Scout camps, and slowly working my way up. My first few camps were one to two nights. Then one was three, then five and now I go to lots of week long camps and I rarely get homesick. To prevent yourself from getting homesick, you can bring a close friend to camp with you, or just find a counselor or parent you like. This way if you do get homesick, you have someone to talk it out with.

BL: Have you ever had a friend stop talking to you for no reason? What did you do?

I have never had this happen to me but, if it happens to you, try to talk to them. If that doesn't work, have someone else talk to them and figure out why they stopped talking to you. Then you can try and solve this problem. Friend drama is the worst, or it seems like it would be!

ASTROCAMP

11~4~16
Astrocamp

As the bus screeched to a stop, my class pressed our faces onto the cool, glass windows. We tried to sneak a peek at what AstroCamp looked like, but our mean bus driver barked at us so we all scrambled back to our seats. I gazed out the window, as rain pelted down. Although it was raining, it was a beautiful sight. I could see the blurry lights or the lanterns hanging from the cafeteria and the silhouettes of deer prancing into the trees while our bus pulled into the lot. AstroCamp was our first field trip of the year and it was for three days! My stomach was already forming a clump of excitement and homesickness at the same time. This trip was about learning about space and our solar system and we get to do a ton of fun activities. To sum up my thoughts I was just all in all excited and nervous about AstroCamp. I wondered if we would get to climb up the power pole that are teacher told us or the zip line, even my brother told me that I get to eat a chip dunked in liquid nitrogen! I really did not know what to think about this trip, but I guess I had nothing to lose.

"Clink!" was the sound of my foot banging on the first hook. "Clink!" was the second. I was trying to climb up a 20 feet tall wood pole and not embarrass myself at the same time, and it was pretty hard! I was wearing a harness that was attached to a metal rope that our instructor was holding. The whole class also had to jump off the pole when they reached the top. I heard my instructors yelling encouraging things like, "Yeah, keep going!" and, "One foot, then the other and the next thing you know you're speeding up the wooden pole!" Sweat was beading down my face, especially because it was the hottest day of the whole trip. I looked down and saw my friends cheering me on, which made me feel a little better. Anxiously I thought, just one more hook! In addition I felt my harness switch gears, I got really scared that I hugged the pole. Finally I got some courage and slid my butt onto the smiley face plate. Next, I stood up slowly and I got in my starting position and then, I just jumped for joy! "Woo hoo!" I shouted. Unsurprisingly, I dabbed for the fun of it and my bunkmates cheered as I spun to the ground. After I was unhooked, I bounced back to my friends and told them, "That was so fun!" and they all laughed.

"Slam!" the door was closed and we were ready to learn. Our group followed our instructors into the classroom and we all sat down on a stool and wondered why there was a vacuum chamber on the desk. Then our instructor explained what we were doing today and why the vacuum chamber was there. "Oh." the class realized. Then we started to talk about gases and different types of planets. There were gas planets and terrestrial planets. Next, we decided to do an experiment. Our instructor put a bowl of liquid nitrogen and put some Lays potato chips in it. Then when the chips froze, he passed them out and told us to pop them in our mouths as fast as we can. So he picked up a chip with a pair of metal tweezers (they started freezing too!) and he dropped one into my hands. I did as he said and popped it in my mouth and chewed. Surprisingly, everyone started laughing at me and I wondered what I was doing wrong, but then I saw smoke coming out of my nose and my mouth and I realized that that was the nitrogen. Then everyone started trying it and smoke came out of their noses too! It was so funny I wish I could've had another.

"Woo hoo!" I was flying like the wind, zipping past the trees, my voice echoed through the bright green forest. I was attached to a zip line and I was spinning and turning and doing all sorts of cool tricks. After all I had done this a few times before. I let go of my harness and put my hands in the air. Then I went a little overboard and tipped over as my shoelaces dangled in my face and

I wondered why my shoes were flying. I then realized I was upside-down so I tipped back up, but suddenly I stopped. I looked around panicking; okay so I was a little scared but you would be to if you were stuck on a zip line and a quarter away from the platform! Thankfully I turned around and saw an instructor with a ball and a rope attached to it, I sighed in relief as she threw the ball towards me. I caught it with two hands and held on for dear life as she pulled me in. "Thank you!" I told her as she unhooked me. "It's okay that has happened to a ton of people." she said. I walked away with a smile on my face. That was the best thing that happened on this field trip! I walked over to my friends and sat down on a log and we chatted on and on about our zip lining experience. We all wished we could do it again, but there's always next time!

As the bus screeched to a stop in front of us, we trudged up the stairs onto the warm pleasant bus and flopped down to our chairs. My class pressed their faces against the cool, glass windows hoping to get a last look at AstroCamp. The bus pulled out of the lot in front of the Cafeteria. I sighed and my breath fogged up the glass, so I drew a face and I laughed. This was a fun trip and I wish it had lasted longer, but nothing lasts forever, right?

- Sadie Joule Som
Age 10

FREYA RUSSELL
LONDON
AGE 14

FLORA
AGE 10

THE SADDEST GIRL IN SPACE-TIME

TRANSMISSION 1
FROM: EARTH DATE JANUARY 1, 2020
TO: EARTH DATE JANUARY 1, 2000

Dear Annamarie,

Hi! It's me, your future self! Don't Panic! This is not a prank and you are not dreaming.

This message comes to you on an important day in your life: the dawn of the new millennium, January 1, 2000.

The scientists responsible for this time-travelling transmission have pinpointed that this is the exact day you need to read this. If this letter comes any later, we fear the best parts of what make you YOU will be swallowed up in favor of "being liked" and "flying under the radar."

And to prevent that happening, these scientists have helped me get the following message to you.

Growing Up is Hard. For Everyone.

The people whose lives you view as "easy" are either really good at hiding it, or will have their trials later.

You, my young little Am, will be very prepared for adulthood for the following reasons: developing way too early, the gap in your teeth, your unibrow (more on that later), people's opinions about your developing way too early, having a gap in your teeth, having a wit that hasn't caught up with your manners, growing up your mother's daughter...and other challenges the scientists have cautioned me against telling you.

Eventually, these things will transform you into a confident, strong woman and a writer who actually has things to write about.

Your life is about to get hard. It will stay that way for quite some time.

But soon, there will be a time where you can choose the things you want and don't want in your life. And that time will be magic.

**Repeat After Me: "Smart is better than pretty. Smart is better than pretty.
Smart is better than pretty."**

Now, this is a tricky one. You'll get a lot of pushback from mom, other girls, boys, teenagers, movies, TV, music...okay, really all media and all people in society.

Basically, as a female, you can't step an inch into this world without being saturated in the "pretty >

smart" culture. And it's not anyone's fault, they're saturated in it, too.

Here's the thing: being pretty doesn't make life easier. Pretty people can still get their arms caught in wood chippers, ride broken waterslides, or unwittingly sit cross-legged on stage during a school play and flash the entire audience (see below).

But if you're smart, all those random happenings are a lot easier to handle.

And I am not saying people can't be smart AND pretty. There are lots of those people in the world. In fact, some may argue that you might even grow up to be one of those people.

But cultivate your smart side first. Invest in the smart.

Smart is active. Pretty is passive.

And if there's anything I can impart to you, Annamarie: do not, dear girl, be passive.

You're Not Broken. Even If The World Is.

Bad things happen. They happen to everyone. Just because they happen to you younger than some, doesn't mean that you're bad, or broken, or that you did anything to cause them.

In fact, when you get to my age, you'll be glad. Not glad the bad things happened, but that bad things made you stronger. And one day you'll look in the mirror and not recoil at your reflection. You'll see yourself as you really are. You'll see a girl/woman who has proven that she can withstand anything and still survive. Still thrive. And there's no better feeling

than that. You'll see.

On Another Subject: Undergarments.

Yay! You got cast in a school play! Congratulations...

Now please wear bike shorts under your dress before you sit with your legs crossed for twenty minutes in front of the entire auditorium. You're welcome.

"No" Is Your Best Friend.

You just don't know it yet. In fact, sorry to call you out, girl, but I know you won't say "no," because you want people to like you. It's okay. Everyone does it. You just might take it a little too far.

Saying "no" will save you from getting roped into toilet papering a classmate's house, getting caught, and getting that scar on your face.

Saying "no" will save you from bad friends, bad situations, and bad people. The only people who won't like you because you have boundaries are the people who just want to exploit your boundaries AKA bad people. Just say "no." It's really fun sometimes. And you may find you're actually quite excellent at it.

"Yes" Is Your Other Best friend.

I know the world is scary when you have an imagination built to find the worse possible outcomes. But staying on the sidelines with your hypothetical safety statistics is boring.

Slide down the waterslide. Waterslides are fun.

There's a lot in life to be afraid of, sure. But there's a lot of fun to be had too, and it usually happens when you do something you haven't done before.

This next one is really important...

Don't Let Mom Wax Your Eyebrows!

The woman is not an esthetician. I know it will hurt when Michael Cabrillo tells you in English class that you have a unibrow. It will hurt because you've picked up on the blatant "different is bad" vibe that, like, the WORLD has.

I know you'll come home crying and beg Mom to help you get rid of your unibrow.

What you really should do is sock Michael Cabrillo in the shoulder and strut down the halls like the bushy-browed mini-goddess you are.

But I get that you might not do that. So, if you must get rid of the unibrow, I beg of you: beg Mom to take you to a professional.

Here's what will happen if you don't: Come home crying. Mom will relent. Then she will bring out The Kit. The Kit is positively medieval. Practically, anyway; it's from the early 1980s. She'll take out a bunch of torture devices as well as some oversized popsicle sticks and misshapen bars of solid amber wax.

She'll melt the wax on the stovetop. It will sting your eyes and smell like burning plastic. You'll sit at the dining room table with a towel over you. She will dip the popsicle stick in the sticky, scalding wax, and spread it on your face. Your face! It will burn. Bad. And just when it stops burning, she'll rip the wax off. It will hurt like no pain you've felt before. And when it stops hurting, it will be too late. Mom will have ripped off half of your right eyebrow. And then, she'll rip off half your left eyebrow to "even things out."

You're going to look "bewildered" for about seven months. I know... "smart is better than pretty." But do you know what else? Natural eyebrows are 100% better than artificial bewilderment.

Being Kind and Being Nice are Two Very Different Things.

Nice is Kind's evil twin. They look alike, but Nice is a silent killer.

Kindness has no ulterior motives. Be kind because it's right. Be kind because it's impossible to tell if someone's in pain. Just by showing a granule of compassion and kindness you can transform someone's day or even their life.

People are nice when they don't want to be honest. Niceness is a coping mechanism for the people who can't say "no" (see above).

Different is Good.

I know that literally everything you see, hear, touch, smell, and taste right now is telling you to be like everyone else. That's just leftover programming from your caveman brain from when you needed societal acceptance to save you from saber-toothed tigers.

It's the new millennia now, saber-toothed tigers are extinct (R.I.P), and different is in. No one ever made history by being the same.

Do you think Marie Curie became the first person to win two Nobel Prizes because she fit in with the girls in P.E. class? No. It's because she studied science at a secret university because it was illegal for women in Poland to go to school. If she'd been the same, she would have died of tuberculosis, in Warsaw. Probably.

And maybe you won't pioneer research on radioactivity (or maybe you will?) But the point is, different people make the world awesome.

So instead of obsessing about why you don't fit in, realize that cool people don't care if they fit in. Annamarie, you're cool because you're convinced you're the reincarnation of a Renoir subject. You're cool because you read. You're cool because you listen to Doo-Wop music. You're cool because you wear tap shoes as regular shoes. You're cool because no one else is you.

You're cool right now. Wanna know how I know? Because one day you'll have a job writing about how cool you were at eleven. Crazy, huh?

In Conclusion (For Now, Because I Have a Lot to Say.)

You may argue that all of these lessons you did eventually learn. You may argue that everything you've gone through has shaped you to be smarter, kinder, and eventually a successful human person; and all that might be true.

I may argue that I used a time travel device to bring you a message from the future and you really shouldn't be arguing.

But of course you are, because you're me.

So, in conclusion, until next time, Little Annamarie:

Kindness: Always (Even to Yourself).

Do Not Be Passive.

It's Okay If Not Everyone Likes You.

The Right People Will Love You.

You're Super Cool. Just As You Are.

And Do Not Let Mom Wax Your Eyebrows.

END OF TRANSMISSION 1.

Written by Annamarie Davidson

BRIGHT LITE MUSIC SPOTLIGHT

DOLLY PARTON

KATHI WILCOX

DEAP VALLY

AN INTERVIEW with DOLLY PARTON

BY EMERY
(AGE TEN)

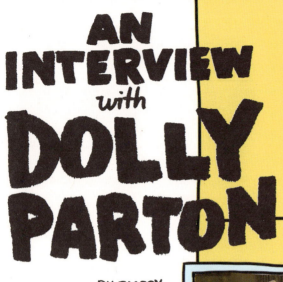

BRIGHT LITE
GIRLZ 4 EVER

Emery: What was your life like as a child?

Dolly: Well Emery, I bet you've read a whole lot about me and my life as a child. My Coat of Many Colors really tells you a lot about it and if you saw the movie you can really see who my parents were and my little brothers and sisters and kind of how we grew up. But my life was good - we were just poor people, just country people, but we had a lot of love and we had Mom and Daddy and we had the woods and the fields to roam in. We had each other to play with so we had so many things that a lot of children don't have a chance to have.

Emery: What inspired you to become a singer?

Dolly: Well, I've always loved to sing. My Mama's people were all very very musical. They all sang, wrote songs, played musical instruments. A lot of them sang in church and a lot of them were just singers, writers. That's who we are as people. Several of my Dad's people used to sing and play but my Mama's people were there so - I was just born into that. They say I came out "Singing and crying in the key of E." But I just loved the music; everything was a song to me. I'd hear the crickets and the rhythm of the fields and the bugs in the fields and I'd start writing songs and get along with the tempo of that. And everything I would hear, I made it into a song. I just had the gift of rhyme. So I just always loved it and even though all my other brothers and sisters were singers and loved to sing, I was the one that really took it to heart. And I would sit around with my guitar writing new songs and learning new songs, thinking about maybe being on the Grand Ole Opry or singing on stage. My Uncle Bill Owens saw that I was really serious about this and so he's the one that helped me get started. It was just my dream, my natural dream.

Emery: What made you choose country music as a genre?

Dolly: Well country music was a natural. What else could I have picked as a genre? Especially growing up back in the Smoky Mountains like that. We didn't have any rock and roll; we didn't even have a TV in my early days. We had radio but most of country people listened to country radio: Grand Ole Opry or the local Farm and Home Hour, where they played the country songs from the country artists. That was the only music we knew at that time so it was only natural that I was a country girl and that I would sing country music. It was only later when I got out in the world and became more of a Town and Country girl that I got to add all those other elements. But that's the great thing about developing as an artist and as a human being. You got to get out of your comfort zone and kind of ease in and out, take chances and do other things. After I felt comfortable with the country music, then I learned to cross over and do the pop music. After I felt comfortable with that, well then maybe I'll do the movies, maybe I'll do this and that. So that's how it goes - it's a progression, life's a progression.

Emery: Are all of your songs auto-biographical?

Dolly: All of my songs are not auto-biographical. They are not all about me, but I love to write other people's feelings. People that I love and know that are going through heartache, maybe divorces or broken hearts that are not able to write about it. I feel so much for them that as a person that can rhyme and can do music, I can take their stories and make 'em my own and feel deep enough about it to where I can write about their sorrows or their happiness. If I see somebody happy - there is a song in my new album called "I Am 16" and I wrote it about one of my sisters that has had a couple of really bad heart-aches in her life. Thought that true love was not for her and she's older now but she met someone and they were just like teenagers. I'd look at them and I'd think, "Look at them; they think they're sixteen." Then I wrote this song and one of the lines is. "...goes to show you're never old unless you choose to be and I will be sixteen forever just as long as you love me." Then it talks about how they really think they're like teenag-

ers again and it goes back. So I just write about my feelings, but so many of my songs are based on truths of my own. There's elements of me in everything, you just have to be smart enough to pick those out. It's like looking for Waldo. (laughs)

Emery: What would you be doing if you were not a singer?

Dolly: If I hadn't been a singer - which I can't imagine that not happening, I think even if I hadn't made it as a singer, I'd still be singing. I'd probably be singing in some night club somewhere. I'd be trying to still get out and sing, even if it was just at the local club or whatever. But even if I'd been singing and hadn't made it, I'd still have to had some kind of a trade to bring in some money so I'd of probably been a beautician. 'Cause I love makeup and hair and I would have gotten a discount on all the makeup and the hair products and the skin products. So that would've been a natural thing. Plus I like to create. I do my own hair. I have a hairdresser of my own but I used to do my hair always. I used to do Mama's hair, my sister's hair. I would fix everybody's hair, 'cause I was good at that. I'd do their make-up. So that would've been a natural thing for me.

Emery: What's your favorite song that you've ever written?

Dolly: I think probably "Coat of Many Colors" is my favorite because it's so much more than a song. It's a philosophy, it's an attitude, it's about my Mom. It's about a way to look at life. There are songs I've written that I enjoy maybe singing more. Like as a singer, "I Will Always Love You" is a great song because you can sing slow and low and then you can sing really big and you know - really show your stuff if you've got a pretty decent voice. There are songs that are more fun to sing as a singer, but I don't think any of them will ever be as personal to me or mean as much as "Coat of Many Colors."

Emery: Have you ever felt insecure in yourself and what inspired you to push forward anyway?

Dolly: Well, everybody has felt insecure and afraid. A lot of people ask me that... Because they say I always seem like I'm not afraid but I've just always said that my desire was greater than my fear. 'Cause anything I wanted to do - of course you get a knot in my stomach, you get scared. Even today, even when I go out on stage, I get that feeling in my stomach. It's not fear, so much as... I don't know what that thing is but, it's just that thing that you know we're human beings. Of course you're gonna - if you got thousands of people out there that are depending on you to do something. I just stand backstage and just ask God to help me, just to show me and let me shine and radiate with his love and light and let me say and do and be something to uplift people, to where we'll all enjoy the evening. So I just really think that you'd have to be not human to not get that element of anticipation and that fear of certain things. I mean I want to do it, and I know I'm gonna do it, but you can't let fear cripple you.

Emery: Do you get nervous before you perform?

Dolly: I don't get nervous. I'm like a racehorse standing backstage in my stall before they let me out. I'm back there stomping around 'cause as soon as I get those butterflies, I get that feeling - and I always try to anchor myself. It's not like a gripping fear for me, it's more of an anxiety. I'm just anxious until I get out there. But the second that light hits me I totally forget everything else and then it's just me and you and God and whatever happens that night. So many wonderful things do happen 'cause I just love what I do and I've never let fear cripple me.

HOW I FELL IN LOVE WITH KATHI WILLCOX

The summer I turned thirteen was the same summer I started wandering over to the local Tower Records. It was in this dead strip mall, a few blocks away from my parents' house, where my musical journey began.

When I was a kid, Towers were everywhere, suburban landmarks. Like Target, Towers had florescent lighting and an impersonal environment. But unlike Target, they only carried DVDs and music.

In an era before smart phones, the only way to see what you were getting was standing tethered to headphones at "listening stations." But the listening stations only played billboard hits or corporate recommendations. You couldn't call to ask a friend. And it wasn't like I had any friends, or cool uncles for the matter, that could have helped. I mean, I had friends - not very many - but I had them. And while they could be described as many things, music connoisseurs they were not. I was alone in this plastic domain of never ending potential mistakes.

Unlike now, buying a record, CD, or DVD in the 90's was like Russian Roulette. Every time you pulled the trigger, you were betting as high as sixteen dollars. Sixteen dollars! For a suburban thirteen-year-old, that's the closest thing you get to betting your life.

WRITTEN BY AMI KOMAI / PHOTOS BY SAMI DRASIN

It was in this deep state of anxiety when I met Kevin and Erica. I was strolling through each aisle, clearly lost and confused when they stopped me to ask if I needed any help. I took one look at them and immediately decided that they were the coolest looking people I had ever seen. I wanted to be just like them. Erica with her perfectly stringy hair gently resting on her shoulders, framing tired and smudged eyes and Kevin with his long hair and dirty white shirt. I loved them.
"I'm not sure," I stammered.
"Are you looking for anything in particular?" Erica asked.
"No," I stupidly said.
And just like that, with a sly smile, Kevin said, "Well, we'll help you then."

Maybe they were bored, maybe they were feeling charitable, or maybe they knew exactly what they were doing: deeply influencing some lucky kid's life. Regardless, whether it was intentional or not, Kevin and Erica opened the door to my musical enlightenment, and I ran through it.

Erica took the lead, and walked me down the aisle.
"B..." she muttered, flipping through CDs. She pulled one out and handed it to me.
"Here. It's Bikini Kill. They're great. You'll like them."
I stared down at the simple black and white cover with the words "The Singles" written across it.
"And it's used. Your lucky day." she said, shuffling the CDs back into place.
"You have no idea," I thought.
Kevin rang me up and I waved goodbye as I ran home with excitement. I burst through my front door and rushed up the stairs, slamming the door closed behind me. As I tore open the sticker seal, I placed the CD into my stereo and pressed play.

Kathleen's voice screamed through the speakers:"I'm the little girl at the picnic who won't stop pulling her dress up. It doesn't matter who's in control now It doesn't matter cuz this is new radio..."

It is not an understatement for me to say that Bikini Kill changed my life.

It is also a fact that Kathi Wilcox was one of the reasons why I chose to play bass. In every band she's in, her bass playing perfectly compliments and anchors the song. Never too flashy and just right. Always the picture image of cool on and off stage.

- Ami Komai

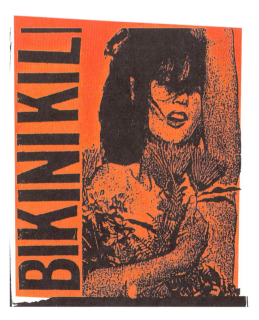

NAME: KATHI WILCOX

HOMETOWN: VANCOUVER
WASHINGTON USA
FAVORITE COLOR: BLACK
FAVORITE FOOD: TACOS
CANT LIVE WITHOUT: BOOKS
HERO: MY MOM
AND ELEANOR ROOSEVELT
FAVORITE PLANET: EARTH
DO YOU BELIEVE IN ALIENS?:
I BELIEVE IN THE POSSIBILITY
OCCUPATION: MUSICIAN

KATHI WILCOX: THE INTERVIEW

Can you give me a little backstory on how your musical career began?

Kathi: There was always a lot of music around my house when I was a kid. I started learning to play violin when I was about 8 or 9, but really didn't like it. I switched to clarinet for a year before finally settling on piano, and pretty much just played piano until I left for college. I think it's good to try a variety of musical instruments if you don't love the first thing you pick up. Later, when I was studying film at the Evergreen State College, I met Tobi Vail and Kathleen Hanna (my future Bikini Kill bandmates). They had both already been in touring bands, but weren't in bands when I met them. We first got together when I was starting my last year of college, so I was 20. Bikini Kill kind of just came together after that, although we didn't have a name for awhile. We practiced and wrote songs in Tobi's parent's garage. I actually didn't know how to play the bass at all when we started, but I did know how to play a few guitar chords. In the beginning it was Kathleen on bass, me on guitar, and Tobi on drums. Billy joined us later,

after we'd already played a few shows. I learned whatever I know about playing bass, guitar and drums by just doing it, playing in lots of bands and with lots of different people, as well as practicing on my own.

How did you end up playing bass?

K: We switched around a lot in the beginning of Bikini Kill. It just ended up making more sense with me on bass and Kathleen singing. Especially after Billy joined the band on guitar. I didn't really understand how the bass worked in songs until I played along with Ramones records. I think it helps when you're learning to find simple music to play along with so you can understand how different kinds of songs are put together. The Ramones are fast, but they don't have a lot of notes. They are easy to figure out. The Beatles are another great band to learn song structure from, but they are a lot more complicated than the Ramones. Especially the bass lines.

Was making music always the priority or

end-game? Or is there a bigger picture for your groups?

K: In Bikini Kill, we wanted to encourage more girls to pick up instruments and start bands. We also wanted women and girls to believe in themselves. Tobi, Kathleen and I all came from feminist backgrounds and our band was a young women's feminist response to '90s American culture, especially underground music at the time. Ultimately we wanted to encourage young women to stand up for themselves, to connect with one another, and to create culture that represented their point of view. The Julie Ruin comes out of a different set of inspirations, maybe more personal issues, but still looks at the world through a feminist lens.

How has your friendship changed over the years?

K: Kathleen and I have been friends for most of our lives at this point. It was hard in Bikini Kill to be close friends because that band was so stressful. She and I became better friends after the band broke up and we moved away from Olympia. I think once we got away from the stress of being in that town and in that band, we were able to appreciate and enjoy each other's friendship a lot more. We've definitely been through a lot together.

What was the most important thing to you as an artist and musician when you started Bikini Kill?

K: Encouraging women and girls to support one another and to express themselves.

Do you still feel that way?

K: Yes. I think some things have changed for the better, but there's so much to be done.

How does music and art have a hand in that vision?

K: I think looking critically at what we consume — music, films, and art -- and asking "what point of view is this reinforcing" is important. Sometimes with pop culture you can get caught up in what your friends are into and not thinking about what it's actually saying, or what YOU think about it. Maybe try seeking out music and art that has a different perspective from the mainstream.

Who were your main influences?

K: My mom is my biggest influence. She was a working single mother when I was young, and she always made time to take us to cultural things like symphonies and art museums. She placed a lot of importance on reading, music, and art - and independent learning in general. I saw how hard she worked to make her life better, while making sure we knew that art, community, and self-expression was important and worth fighting for. She was also a feminist, but I'm not sure I ever heard her call herself that back then.

If you could go back in time, what would you do differently?

K: I would work harder in school. I always got good grades, but I definitely didn't push myself. I suffered from "lazy smart kid" syndrome. I know that's not a very punk rock answer, but it's an honest one.

If you could tell the 13 year old Kathi one thing, what would it be?

K: Trust yourself, go with your gut, and don't worry about what your friends think. I had some crummy "friends" when I was 13 and it took me a long time to break up with them. It was hard at the time but ultimately it was for the best, and I met other friends in high school who ended up being way more interesting, supportive, and cool.

Any advice for aspiring musicians?
K: Follow your own interests and don't worry what other people think. Trust yourself.

Written by Ami Komai

DEAP

LINDSEY TROY
(guitar, vocals)

Rikki: When did you start playing music?

Lindsey: I started playing piano when I was four years old.

Julie: I probably started playing violin when I was six. That must have been the first thing.

Lindsey: Bring that back out.

Julie: I mean, I don't think I can play like that. I could play Twinkle Twinkle Little Star out of key. (laughs)

Rikki: When you were little what did you see yourself being when you grew up?

L: A rockstar or a movie star.

J: Forensic Pathologist.

Rikki: Cool. I'm really into Forensic Files (T.V. show).

J: Cool! I've seen all of them. In fact, when we were in Germany, they had Forensic Files overdubbed in German but it was called something else... I can't remember what it was called but I was like, "Oh I know this one!"
Like, here's a way for me to learn German because I know what happened here!

L: I also would fantasize about being a secret spy. Like Angelina Jolie in Tomb Raider. Like a CIA spy would be super rad.

Rikki: What women inspire you?

Lindsey and Julie: Miranda July, Beyoncé, Amy Schumer, Broad City girls, Peaches, Hillary Clinton

Rikki: Do you believe in aliens?

J: I don't know. If I said "no" it might offend them (the aliens)

L: I don't not. Sure, there can be aliens out there. I don't have any, like, well-developed theories about them. There could be life out there.

J: There's definitely life out there. Whether it be the kind that we all know and love or...

L: Like bacteria?

J: Yeah, bacteria or like weird energy... OR we're the aliens. Like we learned to time travel.

L: There's got to be something out there. At least I hope so. Because once we self-destruct, theres got to be some other life.

J: Also in the ocean – that's where all the craziest aliens are.

Rikki: What would you bring on a trip to the moon?

J: Trip to the moon. I mean there's so many things you would need. I guess I would probably need chapstick on the moon. And wet wipes.

L: Yeah. I'd probably bring like tweezers and a cuticle trimmer. That would occupy my time.

Rikki: What do you find most interesting about space?

J: I'm really into inner space right now because I just had a baby. And speaking of aliens - its like this baby in the inner space of your body.

J: The silence and the distance.

L: The lack of gravity. It's honestly kind of horrifying.

Rikki: What's your favorite food?

L: Refried beans

J: Coffee probably

↑ JULIE EDWARDS
(drums, vocals)

WALLY

LINDSEY TROY AND JULIE EDWARDS

JULIE EDWARDS
(drums, vocals)
→

ARE THE LOS ANGELES ROCK DUO BEHIND DEAP VALLY

LINDSEY TROY
(guitar, vocals)

AMANDA BURCH AGE 14

SPEED LIMIT 18,000

AMANDA BURCH AGE 11

Rooms

Khefri

Asha

Emery

KHEFRI'S
ROOM

CRE·A·TIV·I·TY
THE USE OF
THE
IMAGINATION
OR ORIGINAL
IDEAS,
ESPECIALLY
IN THE
PRODUCTION
OF AN
ARTISTIC
WORK.

GOOD
VIBES

1. What is your favorit thing about your room?
My favorite thing about my room is my bed because it's so comfy! As soon as I walk in, I get the urge to run up to it and flop down onto my pillows and comforter! I also LOVE, LOVE, LOVE the wild mustang print above my desk from my dad's company, Natural Curiosities. I feel like the horse is speaking to me through its eyes. It's so beautiful!

2. What is the one thing you would change about your room? I really love my room. My parents just redid it (as a surprise) for my birthday last month, so it all feels pretty new and exciting. If I could add something, it would be a larger closet, but I'm fine just the way it is.

3. If you could share your room with one person, who would it be? I would share my room with any of my three sisters. I love them all and it's too hard to choose just one! They can take turns being my roomie!

4. If you were to chose one word to describe your room, what would it be?
Magical. Or Dreamy.

5. If you were to chose one word to describe how your room makes you feel, what would it be? One word that describes how my room makes me feel is happy. I instantly feel joyful to be in my room. It's my sanctuary.

ASHA'S ROOM

Bright Lite

1) what is your favorite thing about your room?

My favorite thing about my room is my desk. I love my desk because it's my private space that I can design however I like. It's a place of my own, where I can draw, write songs and do my homework.

2) what is the one thing you would change about your room?

I would take out the television. We don't really need it and it's a distraction.

3) if you could share your room with one person, who would it be?

Besides my sister, I would share my room with my Aunt Shani. Shani is lots of fun, she likes to play dress up and she lets us use her make up and put on fashion shows. Shani also makes the best hot chocolate.

4) if you were to choose one word to describe your room, what would it be?

Fun. There is lots to do in my room. I'm never bored. I can make music, sing, dance and be silly, or draw, or read, whatever I feel like.

5) if you were to choose one word to describe how your room makes you feel, what would it be?

Cozy. My room is not too big, or too small, it's just right.

EMERY'S
ROOM

Photography by Darcy Hemley

1. What is your favorite thing about your room?
My "Tiny Things Collection" and my Potions. The Tiny
Things Collection is an old type tray that has my collection
of tiny, very special things I have found. There are shells,
glass, nests, lizard skin (!), crystals and all sorts of tiny trea-
sures and I use them with my "Potions" which I make with
glitter, essential oils and magic spells I cast. Clare Crespo
gave me the idea for the tray and I've been collecting ever
since!
2. What is one thing you would change about your room?
I would paint my walls lavender and my ceiling dark
purple.
3. If you could share your room with one person who
would it be and why?
I would share my room with my best friend, Lucia because
she is great company and is a very sympathetic and kind
person.
4. If you were to use one word to describe your room what
would it be?
Magical
5. If you were to choose one word to describe how your
room makes you feel, what would it be?
Inspired!

TINY THINGS
COLLECTION

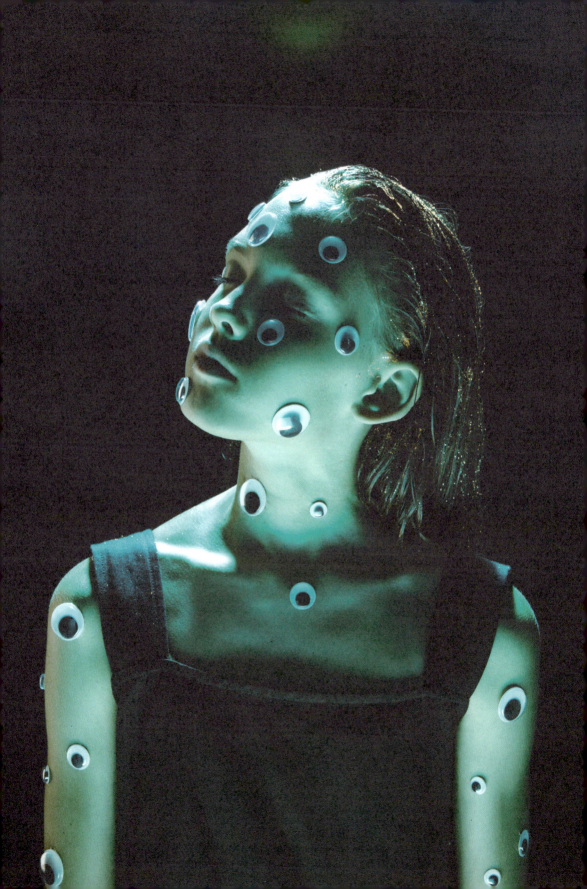

PHOTOGRAPHY
CHRISTA RENEE

ART DIRECTION
MEGHAN KERR

HAIR AND MAKEUP
STEPHANIE PETERSON

STYLING
COLEEN PHELAN

READING LIST BY LIBRARIAN LIZ GORALKA

When You Reach Me,
by Rebecca Stead

After discovering a series of mysterious notes penned by an unknown sender, Miranda gradually realizes whoever is leaving them knows nearly everything about her. including things that haven't even happened yet. With each message she comes closer to believing that she's the only one that can prevent a tragic death—if it isn't already too late.

Stargirl,
by Jerry Spinell
Like an alien dropped down to earth, the arrival of Stargirl at Meca High bursts the quiet conformity of campus and captures the attention of the entire student body. With just one smile, Stargirl also captures Leo Borlock's heart. Once celebrated for being different, Stargirl finds herself shunned for her uniqueness. Desperately in love and anxious to protect her, Leo urges Stargirl to become everything she's not—normal.

Why We Live Where We Live,
by Kira Vermond
Illustrations by Julie McLaughlin

Just how'd we end up here anyway—planet Earth that is! Explore the how's and why's of human existence with Kira Vermond's sweeping study of space and location. Get all the facts, while enjoying colorful illustrations which breakdown the various factors that influence the places humans pick to call home.

Almost Astronauts: 13 Women Who Dared to Dream
by Tanya Lee Stone

Twenty years before the first women were accepted into NASA's space program, thirteen women, known as the "Mercury 13," passed all three phases of the physiological tests NASA required of participants. Despite being accomplished aviators and completing the same tests as their male counterparts, an unspoken rule that astronauts must be white males, barred the Mercury 13 from admittance into NASA's astronaut program. In hopes of one day flying into space, the Mercury 13 publicly challenged the government in addition to perceptions of what women were capable of, paving the way for women in space. Almost Astronauts is a testament to the pioneering woman of the space age and an inspiration for girls interested in studying science and math.

Interstellar Cinderella
by Deborah Underwood
Illustrations by Meg Hunt

Blast off with Interstellar Cinderella, a mechanically inclined girl with pink hair that dreams of repairing rocket ships! Thanks to her pet robotic mouse and fairy god-robot, Cinderella is ready for the ball. But an unexpected mechanical glitch occurs, testing all of Interstellar Cinderella's mechanical expertise!

Ada Twist, Scientist,
by Andrea Beaty, illustrations by David Roberts

Ada Twist may be a girl of few words, but that doesn't stop her from constantly exploring. Ada approaches her surroundings with brazen curiosity, embarking on fact-finding missions and scientific experiments to understand what her world's all about. When a horrific stench fills her home, Ada makes it her mission to find the cause. But Ada's experiments result in an even stinkier-stink, getting her into a whole mess of trouble.

Space! The Universe as You've Never Seen It Before, by DK

Explore the wonders of the cosmos with this comprehensive guide. Bursting with incredible facts, NASA images, and computer-generated 3D models, this book turns a regular kid into a space expert!

Zita the Spacegirl
by Ben Hatke

The push of an all-too-conspicuous little red button propels Zita on a cosmic adventure, where she finds herself a stranger on a bizarre planet. When her best friend Joseph is abducted by an alien doomsday cult, Zita launches a quest to rescue him, unexpectedly making her an intergalactic hero. Feel Zita's shock as she encounters humanoid chickens, neurotic robots, and aliens of various shapes and sizes, thanks to Ben Hatke's incredible illustrations of his zany graphic novel.

Junk Drawer Physics: 50 Awesome Experiments that Don't Cost a Thing
by Bobby Mercer

Jump into scientific exploration with 50 hands-on experiments that make use of the "junk" you already have! Create your own pin hole camera with a paper cup or a star gazer out of repurposed paper towel tubes—all while learning the science behind your discoveries.

A Wrinkle in Time
by Madeline L'Engle

After the mysterious disappearance of her father, Meg Murry encounters an unearthly visitor that shares a cryptic message. Desperate to find her father, Meg delves into his scientific research, discovering his experimentation with the fifth dimension of time travel. With her friend Calvin and brother Charles Wallace by her side, Meg embarks on an astonishing adventure, confronting unknown perils as she travels through the fabric of space and time.

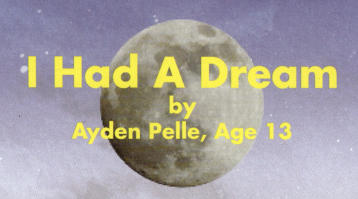

I Had A Dream
by
Ayden Pelle, Age 13

I had a dream. Where I was floating, drifting and soaring towards the unknown. Watching the city become a lighted silhouette and the nightly traffic cacophony dissolve into stillness. I see the painted sunset resting into the mountains peak while the lustrous moon begins its nightly reign. The clouds become dark from a vibrant coral to simple gray, separating from thick crowds to a mere sheet. The stars have come, thank goodness, I was afraid of the prevailing darkness. Now, instead of a city of lights, it is a continent, shining brighter than ever. I see Africa, Asia and Europe, the sights I am seeing are more than imaginable. The earth comes into focus as I now realize the sun rising from its slumber saying good morning to Australia and Taiwan. The moon is now just a large rock drifting in orbit, there is no power in it but the power to deceive. The sun has grown and blinds my glassy, hazel from the sweltering heat. I feel like a marshmallow ready for the s'more.

Now I am past. Mercury lies ahead and Venus too. I soar past the blue planet until I come across Mars and Jupiter. Jupiter, king of the planets towers of the rest. Then, Saturn, my favorite, its halo of rock and dust, who was to say. Its been hours, a while since away from home. I now realize that the stars around me aren't stars at all, but millions of galaxies, a speckled chandelier with the most priceless gems. I now understand how small I am in comparison, how insignificant I am. What lies ahead, what is there to discover? How lucky I am to have seen this - but wait, this is just a dream. Because now I wake to the sun; how small it seems, and the moon; small and unmotivating. Its only now I think how grateful I am to be living the life I am. But where do dreams like that come from? I guess I'll have to find out for myself. And my eyes close to slumber into the Saturday morning sun.

NTERVIEWS

SKATING IN SPACE WITH SIERRA PRESCOTT

BY OLIVE

Olive: How old were you when you started skateboarding?

Sierra: I got my first skateboard when I was in second grade—your age! My grandma got me my first board, it was an Element. I just started skating, honestly, with all the boys. No girls really skated when I was little.

Olive: Did boys ever tease you?

Sierra: They did, until I got better. The best way to quiet people who are being mean is to just outperform them. Just keep doing it, keep learning new tricks, and when they say, "Ahhh, you can't skate!" be like, "If I can't skate, then why am I kickflipping?"
But really, it doesn't matter what anybody says. You should just skate for you.

Olive: What made you want to skateboard?

Sierra: I think it started with this show called Rocket Power. There was a group of kids...it looked so fun. They did all of the board sports.They surfed, snowboarded, and of course they skateboarded. They did all of these big ramps. It was a bunch of boys, and then the sister. I was like, "That is one cool crew!" I wanted it, I wanted to be in that crew.

Olive: What tips do you have for young girl skateboarders?

Sierra: Well, the biggest thing with skateboarding is you've got to commit to it. If you're trying to learn a trick or something, you're not going to actually learn it unless you commit to it. Which means, you need to believe that you can actually do it. You need to think about

it, and tell your board what to do. The more you think about it and actually feel the tricks happening, they're going to happen.

Olive: Who is your biggest inspiration?

Sierra: I have two. The first one is Rodney Mullen. He's a pro skater who started in the 80's, and he just has the most unique style that I've ever seen. He does all of these really crazy flat ground tricks that you've probably never even seen before. He's one of my favorites because of his creativity. And then Jay Adams. He was one of the first guys who brought skateboarding to life in California, in Venice Beach. He did all of the pool stuff, he was a pool shark. Grinding along the side, getting 7 feet over the top, going super fast, sometimes without shoes on. He was an incredible guy.

Olive: Where is your favorite place to skateboard?

Sierra: Definitely the beach. There's something about the smooth pavement, the sand on the sidewalk, the sound of the waves, the wind from the ocean, your hair goes all crazy, it's just really fun. I love when my hair's flying around when I skate.

Olive: What do you do in your free time?

Sierra: Skateboard, eat, cook, explore new places, go to the beach. I'll go to the beach, skate the alleys or beach paths or whatever and just stop for some food. That's like, the perfect day.

Interview by: Olive Weier, Age 7
Photographed by: Alyson Aliano

SPACE! A NEW PLACE TO SKATE

RAD

Collage by: Erin Bates

MIRANDA JULY IS AN AMERICAN FILM DIRECTOR, SCREENWRITER, ACTOR, AUTHOR AND ARTIST.

A CONVERSATION WITH MIRANDA AND STELLA

Stella: What fascinates you most about space?

Miranda: I don't think I've ever been asked that in my life. (laughs)
It is interesting.
Is it fascinating to you?

Stella: Yes.

M: Well, I am always definitely interested if I see an article that says they've made progress in the search for new beings in the universe.

Stella: Like new discoveries about space?

M: Yeah. I guess I think, at a certain point we are going to get way more information. I just feel like, at a certain point they are going to tell us, "They are on this planet and they look like this." And our minds are going to be blown forever. (laughs) And I know that some people say they might be microscopic. But I don't know. I think they will have many arms and many legs and many heads.

S: Do you ever feel inspired by the sky or by space?

M: Yes. Especially the moon. My son has the It's a Small World record that he plays on his record player. It has this line, "There's just one moon." And when I listen to it, it makes me think of how really amazing that is - "There is just one moon." And then I start to think about if I was on other planets, there are many moons! And my question is: If the moon makes gravity, on other planets like Jupiter or Uranus, are you pulled in many directions? Does gravity exist in a different way?

S: When you were younger, did you ever dream about going into space?

M: I think it always seemed really scary. Often when I am going on a trip - like I'm going to London on Saturday - I feel like I'm going to another planet. It's hard for me to imagine, people who actually go into space. It seems like they always have a spouse and children and its just like, "How could you do that?" To go that far away and leave the planet.

S: Right now I'm reading The Martian and all the crew members have wives and children and it's just...

M: I know... choices I guess. They made that choice.

S: Yeah.
Is there a favorite constellation of yours? Is there a memory or a thought attached to that?

M: I always look for Orion's belt. It's three stars in a row. Maybe because its the only constellation I know.

S: Me too. I always look for three stars in a row. But I didn't know that that was Orion's belt.

M: Yeah. I should say now that my dad, wrote a book called... hold on... Where is it?
(Flips through pages)
Called The Night Sky.
This actually isn't the right version but there was a version that came out when I was a child. It's all about the night sky and you would think that I would know more about Orion's belt because my dad wrote a book about it but, I don't.
(laughs)

When I was your age, and the face on Mars was discovered, my dad published the book called The Face on Mars. In fact, the guy, his last name was Hoogland... I can't remember his first name... finished that book in our house.

This guys was living in our house finishing this book because he needed a place to live or something...
You know how sometimes you can feel embarrassed by anything that has to do with your parents? It was embarrassing when kids would joke about The Face on Mars and I would be like, "I don't know what that is. I don't know anything about that." Even though I knew all about it. And even now, I remember the phrase and how people would always say, "It's just a trick of light and shadow." And I always thought that was a really interesting phrase. Isn't everything a trick of light and shadow?
(points to page)
And there it is. It looks a lot like a face but I guess...

S: It kind of looks like David

Bowie's face.

M: Oh yeah... I can see that.
What if that's a major discovery?

S: (laughs)
Next question.
Well, this one's probably the weirdest question. What do you think space smells like?

M: Oh. Wait. I think I read this... I guess I'm picturing what ozone smells like... not that I know what that smells like but, now I'm picturing a hairspray can because of the aerosol. Like an empty hairspray can. (laughs)

S: I think space smells clean. like cleaning products but not the scented ones. Like Borax.

M: Oh yeah. That's a good one.

S: I mean Borax doesn't really smell like anything but it smells a little bit like... Borax.

M: Did you see The Martian or are you just reading it?

S: I saw it and then I wanted to wait before I read so I would

forget it.
Did you like The Martian?

M: Yeah, I did.
I mean. I found it a little bit unbelievable towards the end when he made it back, basically flying on a paper bag but...

S: I like space, its interesting in general but I liked how when he was alone, he became really sarcastic and it was funny how he was stuck in space but he was still making jokes.

M: It's sort of like, that's what saves him.

Interview by Stella Bonstin, Age 11

MUFON

Debbie Ziegelmeyer
Imperial, Missouri
Mutual UFO Network

Missouri MUFON State Director,
MUFON Star Team Investigator,
Director of the MUFON Dive Team
MUFON Business Board of Directors

BEFORE I even knew what a UFO was, I was just a six year old girl, crying on the kitchen floor. In school earlier, I'd learned that cats only see in black and white. I sobbed, trying to clutch my tabby cat Muffin in my arms, as she scuttled away under the stove to seek refuge from my wailing.

"It isn't fair!" I cried, mourning every color Muffin didn't even know she couldn't see.

Joe, my mother's boyfriend at the time, a kind man who owned horses and always smelled faintly of green hay, knelt down to comfort me. When I explained why I was so sad, he asked me, "Says who?"

"Scientists," I answered, my breath choking in my throat.

"Okay, but how can they possibly know that?"

I was perplexed for a moment, 'til he finished.

"Have these scientists ever been a cat?"
"No…"
"So how can they possible know what cat can or can't see?"

Something momentous happened to me that day. Joe taught me that just because someone tells you something is true, it doesn't mean it is. And ever since then, I've been the kind of person who's looked at the world with a sense of wonder. The kind of person who doesn't just ask, "Why?" but also asks, "Why Not?"

I was reminded of this lesson when researching the Mutual UFO Network, or MUFON. A wild curiosity overtook me as I explored the expansive collection of case files their website has to offer.

MUFON has been around to question what we've been taught since 1969; the same year the USA put the first man on the moon.

They not only question, they examine. This includes the flying saucers, crop circles, and alien technology. But I was surprised to find articles to do with subjects like higher dimensions,

ancient astronauts, and time travel.
The kind of things that read like science fiction, MUFON hopes to make science fact.

I have to admit, I was skeptical. I thought I was going to look into a world of kooky, conspiracy theorists, regardless of how fascinating their lives and ideas might be.

But I was wrong. MUFONs field investigators are distinguished, highly educated people. They use the Scientific Method, a rigorous process that has been used by scientists for hundreds of years to discover the unbiased truth. And a lot of MUFONs members are scientists themselves! Theses members aim above all else to "discover the true nature of this phenomenon."

Seem crazy? Probably. But in the age of pocket technology, the race to Mars by privatized companies like Space X, and living in an ever expanding universe, isn't this the time, more than ever, to accept that we still have so much more to discover?

Debbie Ziegelmeyer, Missouri State Director of MUFON and Star Team Investigator indulged my curiosity and sense of wonder.
And whether you believe in aliens or you don't, you at least have to be open to the possibilities.

Because, again, why not?

Annamarie: First off, please tell us a little about yourself and your background.

Debbie: I joined MUFON in 2000. I have investigated over 1000 sighting reports including 710 MUFON cases. As a Scuba Instructor, I am also a key expert for underwater UFO/USO Search and Recovery. I became a 1947 Roswell, NM Crash Investigator in 2001 participating in archeological onsite digs in 2002 and 2006. I have also done research into alternate Roswell 1947 (UFO) crash sites and have interviewed multiple witnesses. In the past 16 years I have appeared as a conference speaker on the subject of Roswell, NM, Missouri UFO sighting reports, and many additional related topics. Missouri is one of the most active areas for UFO sightings in the United States.

A: Your official MUFON title is Star Team Investigator. What does that mean? And is it as interesting as it sounds?

D: MUFON Star Team Investigators are MUFON's most experienced Field Investigators. They are Investigators who own their own investigating high-tech equipment including Geiger counters, night vision binoculars and cameras, EMF meters, etc. They are highly skilled and trained in physical evidence recovery and witness interview skills.

A: Do you prefer the term aliens, extraterrestrials, or is there another term you use?

D: I prefer the term extraterrestrials or other worldly life forms.

A: Were you always interested in aliens and outer space? Was there a specific moment that made you say, "This is what I want to do"?

D: I grew up a "Star Trek" and "Lost in Space" (TV program) child, who watched the night sky from a small Arizona town and always owned her own telescope. I currently own a Schmidt Cassegrain 10" mirror telescope which is housed in a 7 foot tall dome in my back yard.

A: We can imagine in your line of work you're met with a lot of skeptics. Were you ever a skeptic yourself? If so, what changed your mind?

D: I am still a skeptic. Every good investigator has to go into an investigation wondering what it was the witness actually saw and how that can be explained. When I run out of possibilities and explanations I can begin a serious detailed investigation into what was reported.

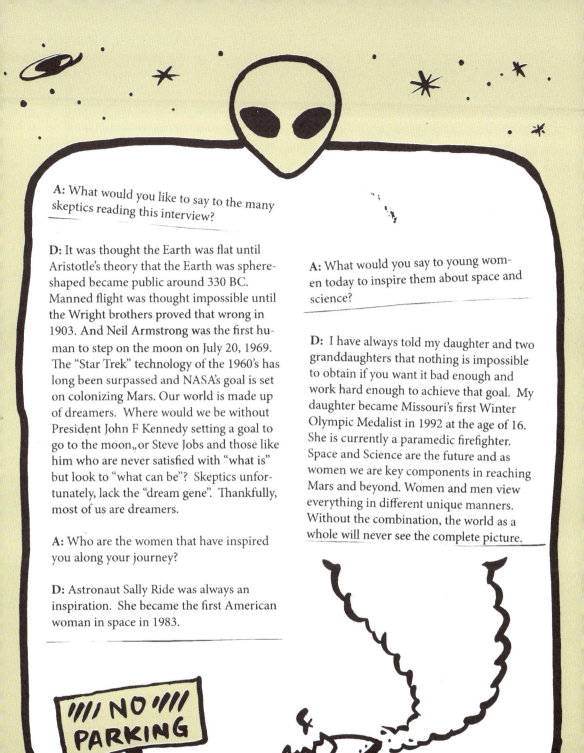

A: What would you like to say to the many skeptics reading this interview?

D: It was thought the Earth was flat until Aristotle's theory that the Earth was sphere-shaped became public around 330 BC. Manned flight was thought impossible until the Wright brothers proved that wrong in 1903. And Neil Armstrong was the first human to step on the moon on July 20, 1969. The "Star Trek" technology of the 1960's has long been surpassed and NASA's goal is set on colonizing Mars. Our world is made up of dreamers. Where would we be without President John F Kennedy setting a goal to go to the moon,, or Steve Jobs and those like him who are never satisfied with "what is" but look to "what can be"? Skeptics unfortunately, lack the "dream gene". Thankfully, most of us are dreamers.

A: Who are the women that have inspired you along your journey?

D: Astronaut Sally Ride was always an inspiration. She became the first American woman in space in 1983.

A: What would you say to young women today to inspire them about space and science?

D: I have always told my daughter and two granddaughters that nothing is impossible to obtain if you want it bad enough and work hard enough to achieve that goal. My daughter became Missouri's first Winter Olympic Medalist in 1992 at the age of 16. She is currently a paramedic firefighter. Space and Science are the future and as women we are key components in reaching Mars and beyond. Women and men view everything in different unique manners. Without the combination, the world as a whole will never see the complete picture.

NO PARKING

Written by Annamarie Davidson

CANCER

SCORPIO

GEMINI

LEO

CAPRICORN

PISCES

VIRGO

SAGITTARIUS

ARIES

TAURUS

LIBRA

AQUARIUS

PLANETS of OUR

EARTH

NEPTUNE

MERCURY

URANUS

VENUS

SOLAR

MARS

JUPITER

SATURN

SYSTEM

COOPER AND CHARLIE'S OUTER SPACE ADVENTURE

By
Kylie Yobe (age 11)

My good friend Cooper and I are going on a space adventure! We got chosen to be the first dogs to go into outer space. Our mission is to land on Neptune and explore to see if there is any life on the planet.

It was finally the day! The day that Cooper and I get to go to outer space.

When I woke up, Cooper said, "Can I sleep in outer space?"

I said, "Probably, but why would you want to sleep at a time like this?" I guess I don't really understand what "SLEEP" means.

When we got to the space station everyone looked like they were ready for us to get on the spaceship already. We hurried to put our spacesuits on and then it was time to enter the spaceship. It was so big I felt like a little ant!

When Cooper and I got inside the ship there was so many buttons I didn't even know where to look. When it was time to go, we strapped on our seat belts and ………….3……….2……….1………. Blast off! We were going to outer space!

The spaceship mumbled and grumbled and pulled us into the air. Soon enough we were on Neptune and it felt like we hadn't eaten in forever so we had some dried up dog food. Mmmmm, that was good!

We looked around for about an hour and saw nothing. Just then we heard a peculiar noise like a "ka ka" but we didn't know where it was coming from. Then right at that moment a bird-looking hybrid came swooping down. It was like a chinchilla mixed with a parrot. It looked scared so we talked for a while and found out that he was a goglaforphin (go/gla/for/fin) bird.

We took him on our spaceship since we didn't want his species to become extinct. After all, he was the last one. That is the story how Cooper and I found our new best friend, Kevin.

(Hey Cooper here. None of that stuff really happened. He has some crazy dreams doesn't he? Alright got to go, peace out fellow pug and lab lovers!)

I WAS THE
SOLAR SYSTEM

BY: DANIELA MARTINEZ AGE 11

In fifth grade I had this brilliant idea for Halloween. My idea was to be the Solar System. When I told my mom about my idea, she said, "It sounds like a great challenge to make it." I was so excited. It was kinda hard to create. We had to figure out how to put all the planets in place and where the sun was going to go. We got help from my family. They helped us by giving us things they didn't use or need anymore to recycle. Another way they helped us was by putting the costume together, and making helpful suggestions to make it better. I was really excited that year to show everybody at school my costume for Halloween, but at the same time I was nervous. When we finished my costume I was so proud of my family and everybody that had helped to make it. I was ready to wear my costume already; I couldn't wait to see everybody's face when I entered school with my costume on me. On the day of Halloween my mom helped me put my costume on. When I was ready to go to school, I went to the car and it was actually a little tricky to get on because my head had a big circle around it as the sun. On my way to school some of the people in other cars turned to look at me and gave me a "thumbs up" or smile. At school many staff and students gave me good compliments about my costume. That day, my class chose me to represent them in the Most Creative Costume category for the school costume contest. When it was time for the contest, I got very nervous because there was some pretty creative costumes right there, like the banana costume. But at the end I still won. I felt really proud of myself and my family. And my class felt proud of me also for being so creative.

I had a wonderful Halloween that year.

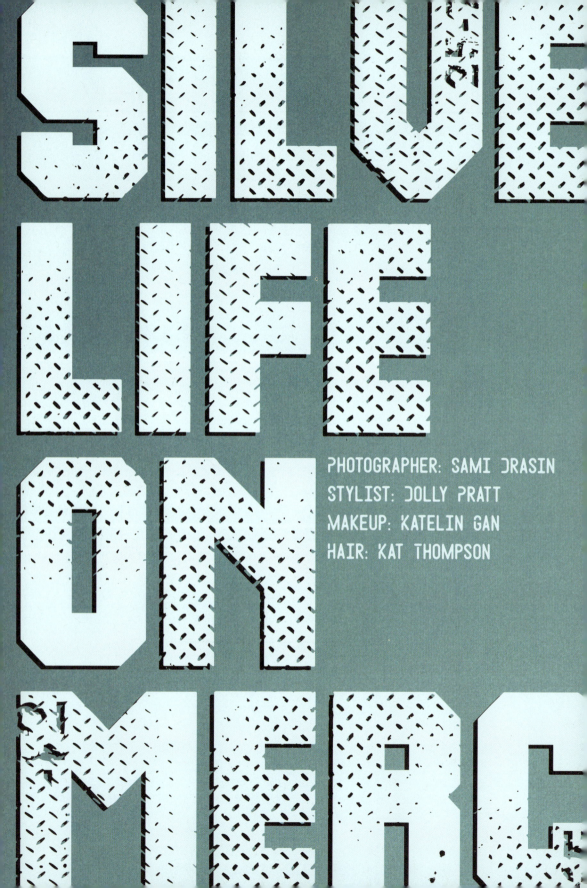

SILVE
LIFE
ON
MERC

PHOTOGRAPHER: SAMI DRASIN
STYLIST: DOLLY PRATT
MAKEUP: KATELIN GAN
HAIR: KAT THOMPSON

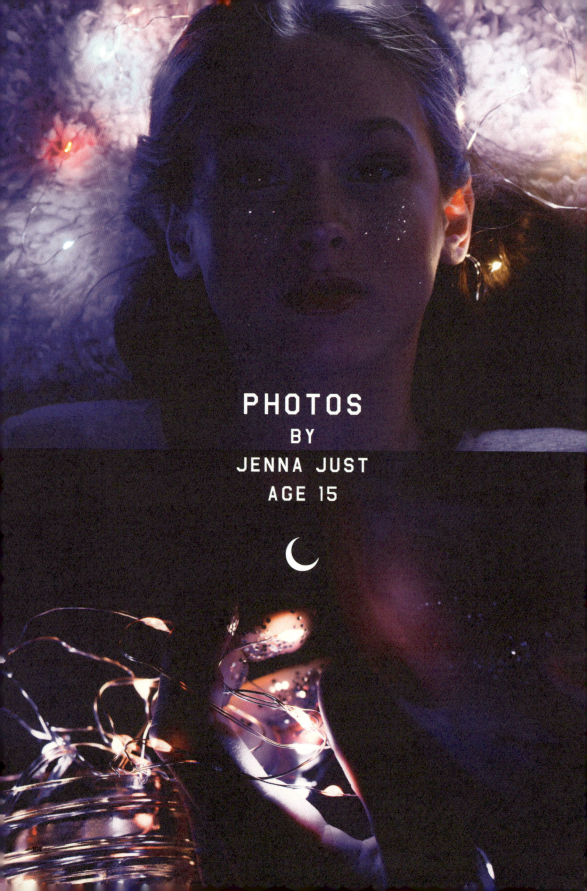

PHOTOS
BY
JENNA JUST
AGE 15

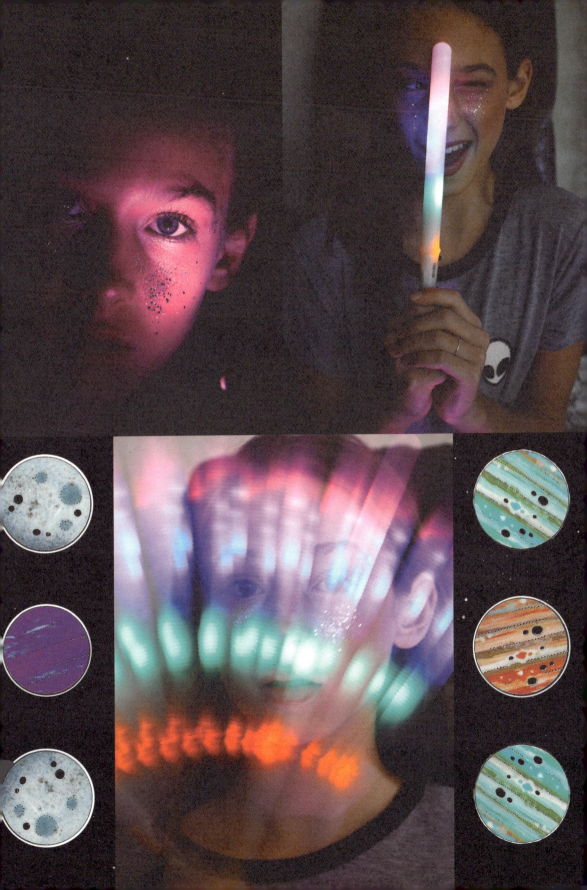

Northern Lights

Photographed by Wesley Pfleeger in Iceland

The bright dancing lights of the aurora are actually collisions between electrically charged particles from the sun that enter the earth's atmosphere. The lights are seen above the magnetic poles of the northern and southern hemispheres.

My Imaginary Planet

Planet Powow is a mythical wonderland. It's full of crazy creatures that work together with love and peace. It's wonderful!

By Lucinda Boys
Age 11

Photographer: Olivia Robinson
(15 years old)
Stylist: Dolly Pratt
Hair: Traci Barrett
Makeup Nathan Hejl

Here's to You...
Sailor

Moon

117

Moon background illustration by Jonathan Dalton

ASTRONAUTS AND COSMONAUTS YOU SHOULD KNOW.

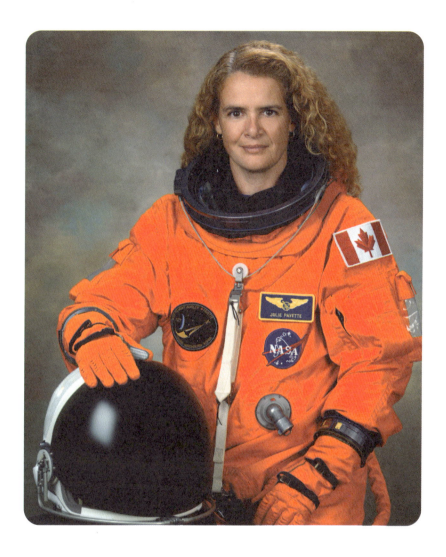

Julie Payette is a Canadian astronaut, engineer and administrator. Julie has completed two spaceflights, and logging more than 25 days in space. She served as Chief Astronaut for the CSA, and has served in other roles for both NASA and CSA, such as CAPCOM.

Kalpana Chawla was an Indo-American astronaut
and the first woman of Indian origin in space. Her first
mission was as a mission specialist and primary robotic arm operator on Space Shuttle Columbia in 1997.
In 2003, Chawla was one of the seven crew members
killed in the Space Shuttle Columbia disaster.

Laurel Blair Salton Clark was an American medical doctor, United States Navy Captain, astronaut and Space Shuttle mission specialist. Clark died along with her six fellow crew members in the Space Shuttle Columbia disaster.

Naoko Yamazaki is a former Japanese astronaut at JAXA, the second Japanese woman to qualify. Yamazaki became the second Japanese woman to fly into space. Naoko was born in Matsudo City, Japan.

Sally Kristen Ride was an American physicist and astro-naut. She became the first American woman in space in 1983 after joining NASA in 1978. Born in Los Angeles, at 32, Sally is still the youngest American astronaut to have traveled to space.

Samantha Cristoforetti is an Italian European Space Agency astronaut, Italian Air Force pilot and engineer. She holds the records for longest single space flight by a woman (199 days 16 hours) and for the longest uninterrupted spaceflight of a European astronaut. She is also the first Italian woman in space.

Fun fact: Samantha is also known as the first person who brewed an espresso coffee in space.

Yi So-yeon is a biotechnologist and astronaut who became the first Korean to fly in space.

Chiaki Mukai is a Japanese doctor, and JAXA astronaut. She was the first Japanese woman in space, and
was the first Japanese citizen to have two spaceflights.
In total she has spent 23 days in space.

Liu Yang is pilot and astronaut and became the first Chinese woman in space on June 16th, 2012. She served as a crew member on the space mission Shen-zhou 9.

Valentina Tereshkova, pilot-cosmonaut, hero of the USSR, was the first female cosmonaut. After being selected on June 16th, 1963 from over four hundred applicants, she completed 48 orbits of the Earth in her three days in space.

Sharon Christa McAuliffe was an American from Concord, New Hampshire, and was one of the seven crew members killed in the Space Shuttle Challenger disaster.

Anousheh Ansari is an Iranian-American engineer, co-founder and chairwoman of Prodea Systems and the first Iranian woman in space. The Ansari family is also the title sponsor of the Ansari X Prize.

Mae Carol Jemison is an American engineer, physician and NASA astronaut. She became the first African-American woman to travel in space when she went into orbit aboard the Space Shuttle Endeavour on September 12, 1992.

Space Treats

By Sera Wilcox

Full Moon Pies
(aka Apple Hand Pies)

YOU WILL NEED:

One package frozen (and thawed) traditional pie dough that has two 9" sheets

(I like the Wholly Wholesome brand, or use your favorite homemade pie dough)

2 large organic green apples, peeled and cored

(Why choose organic? Apples are number two on the "dirty dozen" list)

2 tablespoons dairy, or non-dairy, butter

1/4 cup cane sugar (or sweetener of your choice, like sucanat or maple sugar)

Small pinch of salt

1 teaspoons ground cinnamon

1 teaspoon water

1 1/4 teaspoon turbinado sugar (for the top)

1 whisked egg (or 1/4 c coconut milk if vegan) to make the crust golden

WHAT TO DO:

Line a baking sheet with a silicone mat or parchment paper.

Cut peeled and cored apples into quarters, cut each quarter into 4 wedges, and cut each quarter into 4 more wedges. This should give you 16 pieces per apple.

Melt butter in a large skillet over medium heat; let butter brown to a light golden color and until butter smells toasted, less than 1 minute. Stir apples into hot butter; sprinkle with a small pinch of salt and cane sugar. Cook and stir apple mixture until apples are softened, about 5 minutes. Mix in cinnamon and water; continue cooking until apples are soft and sticky, 1 to 2 more minutes. Spread apple filling onto a plate to cool.

Preheat oven to 400 degrees.

On a lightly floured work surface, unroll the pie dough sheets and cut each sheet into four circles using a 4" cookie cutter. Combine the left-over dough into a ball, reroll to the same thickness as the other circles and make 2 more circles. One box of dough will make ten circles, which will then make 5 hand pies.

Spoon 6 cooked apple pieces in the center (don't worry if it broke or mushed, it will still look and taste great), leaving about ¼" of space around the edges. Cut 3 small holes ("moon craters") in the top piece of dough and place on top of the bottom one with that has the apples (it's ok to stretch it gently to fit over the apples. Carefully press dough closed around filling, using a fork and place the 3 cut-out pieces on top covering half of each apple hole and wherever you wish.

Repeat with remaining dough and filling. Transfer pies onto prepared baking sheet.

Whisk egg with milk in a small bowl until thoroughly combined. Brush top of each hand pie with egg mixture (or coconut milk if vegan) and sprinkle with about 1/4 teaspoon of turbinado sugar.

Bake in the preheated oven until pies are golden brown and filling is bubbling, about 20ish minutes. The key is that the pies look golden and smell delicious. Take out and let cool for at least 15 minutes before serving. *Check that you turned off the oven ;).

In the summer try making these stellar pies with peaches or apricots!

Venus
Veggie
w/Hum

Alien Lemonade

YOU WILL NEED:
2 quarts cold sparkling water
½ cup lemon juice (about 4-6 fresh lemons depending on their size. You can use limes, too!)
¼ to ½ teaspoon pure stevia powder
½ teaspoon Spirulina powder

WHAT TO DO:
Juice the lemon with a juicer and pour into a large jug.

Add ¼ teaspoon stevia and the spirulina and whisk well to combine.

Pour in sparkling water and stir if needed to mix and adjust stevia sweetness to desired taste.

Serve straight away (over ice is nice).

Moon Pies!

MAN-IN-
THE-
MOON

Moon
Rocks
(popcorn)

Moon Rocks
(aka Honey Caramel Popcorn Balls)

YOU WILL NEED:

10 cups plain popped popcorn (choose Non-GMO if possible)

(FYI, if you pop your own popcorn, ½ cup of kernels = about 10 cups popped corn)

3/4 cup brown sugar

1/3 cup honey

2 tablespoons butter (use earth balance or coconut oil if vegan)

WHAT TO DO:

Measure the popcorn into a large bowl (discard any unpopped kernels that settle at the bottom if you popped your own), then melt the butter, sugar and honey in a small saucepan over low heat until the mixture is uniform, stirring constantly (about 5 to10 minutes max).

Pour the caramel mixture evenly over the popcorn. Toss the popcorn with two spatulas or large spoons until coated. At this point, you can add an optional 1 cup of mini marshmallows (or ½ cups nuts, dried fruit, chocolate chips, ½ teaspoon cinnamon, etc.) and mix well.

Once the caramel has cooled enough to touch (about 5ish minutes)– the popcorn is ready to shape into balls. Use your hands to shape your moon rocks. By keeping a layer of plastic wrap between your hands and the popcorn mixture you'll avoid a sticky mess. Use as much pressure as you need to form the popcorn mixture into balls. Note: You can reuse the one piece of plastic to shape your balls over and over to be kind to the environment. When finished shaping, wrap each in foil to create your out-of-this-world treat. Rock on!

Makes about 10 (depending on the size you shape)

Photography by Christa Renee

HOW TO :
BUILD A SPACE MOBILE, STARRY NIGHT JEANS, STAR SHOES , AND SPACE FABRIC

Supplies:
· Plain white sneakers
· Black spray paint
· Paint (different blues, purple, red, pink, & white)
· Glow in the dark paint
· Glitter
· Paint Brushes
· Sponge
· Blow dryer

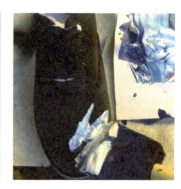

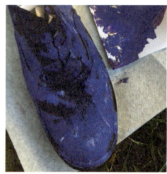

DIY STAR SHOES

BY GEORGIA GOODMAN AGE 10

1. Spray paint your shoes black. I used a blow dryer to dry them so I could continue making the shoes in a short period of time, but you can also let the shoes dry for a few hours.

2. Then mix up all your different color paints to get a color that reminds you of the galaxy. I mixed all of my paints, and added white to blend it.

3. Now, you can paint the shoes with a brush or use a sponge to blot the shoes all over. You should have a few different blues all over the shoes like lighter and darker spots. You can also add little spots of glow in the dark paint all over to look like stars when you are in the dark.

4. Next, I sprinkled glitter all over the shoes before the paint dried. I used the blow dryer again to dry the glitter and paint.

5. Voila, you have some super cool intergalactic shoes!

DIY SPACE MOBILE

BY FRANCES

WHAT YOU NEED:
CARDBOARD
ACRYLIC PAINTS
PAINTBRUSHES
HOLOGRAPHIC STICKER PAPER
GLITTER TAPE

Make a cross out of cardboard. To do this we cut 2 pieces of equal length and width shapes - approx 12" long by 2.5" wide shapes. We fashioned one shape into a shooting star and the other into a crescent moon.

To make the cross shape, we made slits/cuts in the middle of each shape and fit the 2 pieces together at the slits, forming an "X". We then strung this up with fishing line and a small plastic washer at the top for a hook. Making the holes in the cardboard cross with a kebab stick.

Then we drew and painted the mobile shapes on cardboard that included planets, stars, rocket ships etc.. Making them different sizes. Then we carefully cut them out with a knife and then painted the other side of them to match. Letting them dry for a few hours.

Once they were completely dry we pierced holes in the mobile shapes with a kebab stick - deciding first where we wanted to place/hang the pieces from the cross shape/structure. Then we took fishing line and threaded them up to the cross structure.

It helps to have a place to hang the mobile whilst you are working on it.
We placed one end of a wood dowel under some heavy books on a book shelf,
so we could hang it from the other end.

DIY STARRY NIGHT JEANS

BY SASHA   AGE 8

*Sasha is an 8 year old girl who has been challenged with Cerebral Palsy since birth. She's on a mission to help raise funds for art therapy programs at Children's Hospital Los Angeles which benefit patients like her. Please visit www.The-SashaProjectLA.org to learn more.

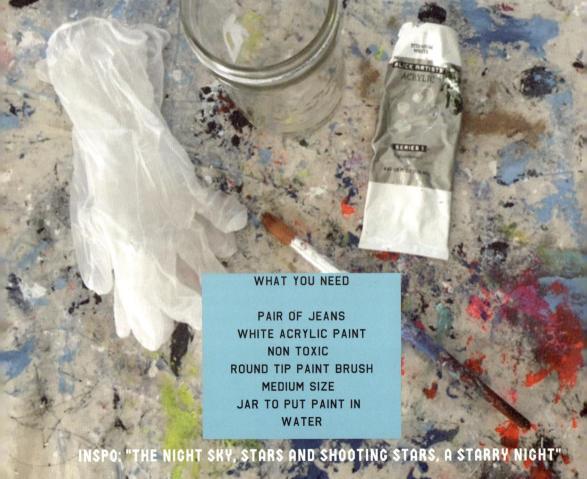

WHAT YOU NEED

PAIR OF JEANS
WHITE ACRYLIC PAINT
NON TOXIC
ROUND TIP PAINT BRUSH
MEDIUM SIZE
JAR TO PUT PAINT IN
WATER

INSPO: "THE NIGHT SKY, STARS AND SHOOTING STARS, A STARRY NIGHT"

DIY INSTRUCTIONS

COMBINE A LITTLE BIT OF WATER AND PAINT IN A GLASS JAR
AND MIX USING THE PAINT BRUSH.
PLACE JEANS ON A LARGE CLOTH OR PAPER.
BE CAREFUL
THIS CAN GET MESSY
DIP THE PAINT BRUSH IN THE JAR WITH THE PAINT.
MAKE SURE THE BRUSH IS PROPERLY SOAKED WITH PAINT
AND START SPLATTERING
LET IT DRY FOR 5 MINUTES THEN TURN OVER TO PAINT /
SPLAT THE OTHER SIDE.

DIY ROTARY PRINTED SPACE FABRIC

BY RIKKI JOHNSON

Brayer>

TOOLS:

- 2 yards blank fabric
- Rolling pin
- Foam sheets with adhesive backs
- Exacto knife
- Scissors
- Brayer (rolly thing)
- Screen printing ink
- Tape
- Sewing machine or needle and thread
- Two large pieces of cardboard

STEP 1:
Remove paper on back of the foam sheets and layer 2-4 pieces directly on top of eachother.
Leave the bottom layer with backing still in place.

STEP 2:
Draw 1 inch space shapes on the top layer.

STEP 3:
Cut foam space shapes out using the exac-to or scissors.

STEP 4:
Remove backing from bottom layer and stick space shapes onto the rolling pin.

STEP 5:
Spread ink on a piece of cardboard with the brayer. On a separate piece of card-board lay a piece of 12 x 12in fabric taping the sides so it won't move.

STEP 6:
Lightly roll the rolling pin in the ink covering all the shapes.

STEP 7:
Roll the rolling pin onto the fabric.

STEP 8:
Decide what you'd like to use your fabric for (They are great for cloth napkins!!) and sew the edges.

COLORING PAGES

PAGES COLORING PAGES

Alexandra Coward

MERCURY

VENUS

EARTH

MARS

JUPITER

SATURN

NEPTUNE

URANUS

Rikki Johnson

Carolyn Kelly

Angela Goleme 169

CRYSTALS

BY WESLEY PFLEEGER AGE 10

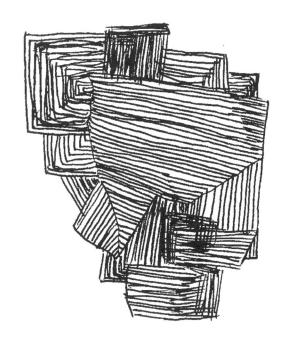

Bismuth

Atomic number: 83.

System: hexagonal.

Bismuth was one of the first
10 metals to be discovered

Bismuth relieves symptoms of
isolation.

In Earth's crust bismuth is about
twice as ubundant as gold

Himalayan
Quartz
Cluster

These quartz clusters grow in the
highest place on earth, and seem to
be a bridge from Earth energy to Air energy
allowing them to be particularly suited
to meditation uses.
They are well formed and very stunning.
Source: Tibet

Uses: Himalayan quarts crystals are
used in meditation to induce a total
centering of one's self, and they produce
an energy conductive to chaneling.

Scolecite

Scolecite is a monoclinic
mineral. it is monoclinic m with
space group Cc, but crystals
are pseudotetragonal. scolecite usally
occurs acicular (needle like) and
fiberous aggregations. Scolecite
commonly occurs as sprays of thin,
prismatic needles, frecently flatened
to one side, with slanted termimations
and striated parallel to the length of
the needles.

Pyrite

The mineral Pyrite, or iron pyrite,
also known as fools gold, is
an iron sulfide with the chemical
formula FeS_2. This minerals
metalic luster and pale brass-Yelow
hue give it a superficial
resemblance to gold.
Pyrite is the most common
of the sulfide minerals.
Iron-Pyrite FeS_2 represents the
prototype compound of the
crystallographic Pyrite stucture.

SPACE FRIENDS
BY: STELLA (AGE 13) AMELIA (AGE 13) CLAIRE (AGE 13) PIPER (AGE 13)

Untitled by Nomi, Age 13
Model: Georgia Wood

PHOTOS...
ELLA VALENSI
TALYA AXEL
LUCIA LENNOX

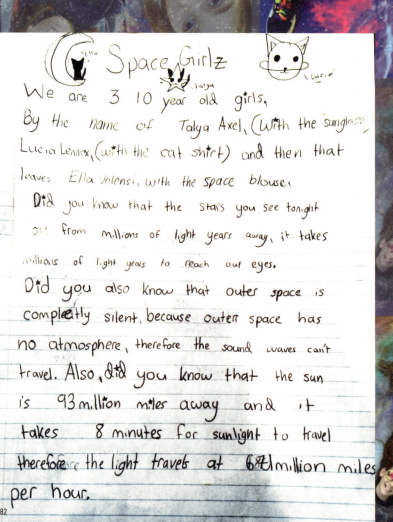

Space Girlz

We are 3 10 year old girls,
By the name of Talya Axel, (with the sunglasses)
Lucia Lennox, (with the cat shirt) and then that
leaves Ella Valensi, with the space blouse.
Did you know that the stars you see tonight
are from millions of light years away, it takes
millions of light years to reach our eyes.
Did you also know that outer space is
completely silent, because outer space has
no atmosphere, therefore the sound waves can't
travel. Also, did you know that the sun
is 93 million miles away and it
takes 8 minutes for sunlight to travel
therefore the light travels at 671 million miles
per hour.

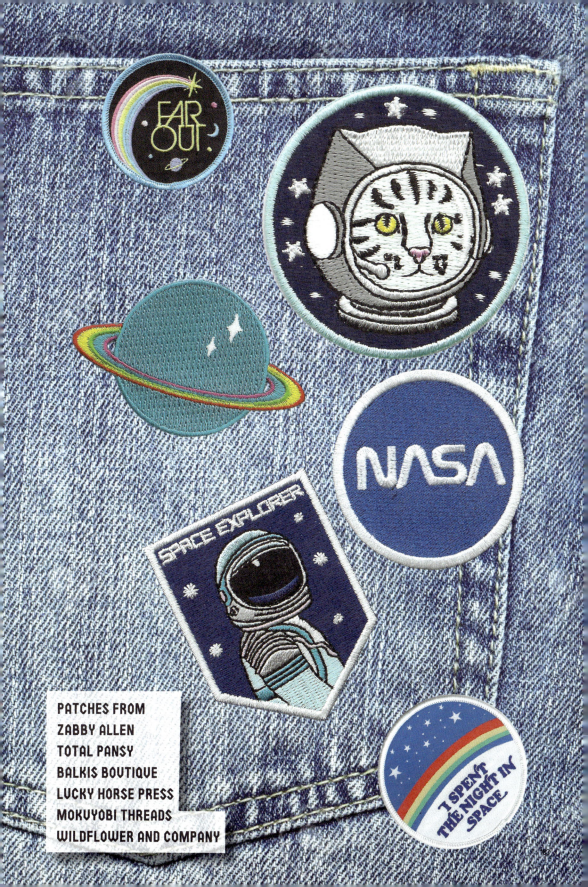

FAR OUT.

NASA

SPACE EXPLORER

I SPENT THE NIGHT IN SPACE

PATCHES FROM
ZABBY ALLEN
TOTAL PANSY
BALKIS BOUTIQUE
LUCKY HORSE PRESS
MOKUYOBI THREADS
WILDFLOWER AND COMPANY

"Do not look at stars as
bright spots only.
Try to take in the vastness
of the universe."

Maria Mitchell,
Astronomer

Maria Mitchell (August 1, 1818 – June 28, 1889) was an American astronomer who discovered a comet using a telescope in 1847.
She was awarded a gold medal from King Frederick VI of Denmark for her discovery and became known as the first professional female astronomer.

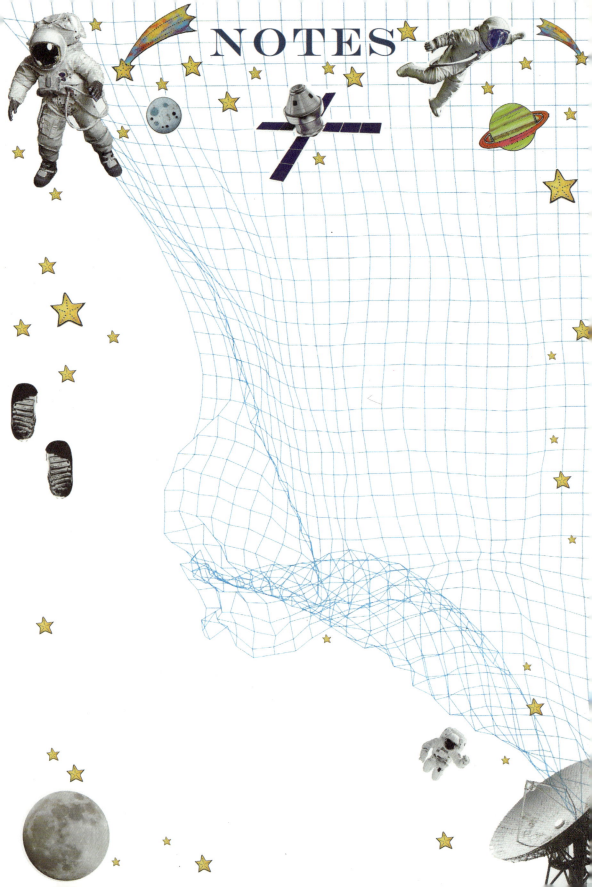

NOTES

NOTES

SUBMISSION CALL!

Our quarterly magazine is a collection of submissions from girls all over the world. Bright Lite includes photography, interviews, articles, recipes, crafts, journals posts, music and advice curated just for them.

Please go to
www.brightlitemag.com/submissions
for submission details.

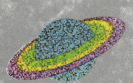

THANK YOU
THANK YOU
THANK YOU
THANK YOU
THANK YOU
THANK YOU
THANK YOU

Thank you to all of our amazing contributors, illustrators, writers, photographers and everyone that supports us. Without you, this magazine would never exist and we are always and forever grateful.

Vida Wang
Rachel Wagner Koppa
Emily Fernandez
C. Bohica
Karin Hoving
Jennifer Pitt
Melody
Amy Law
Kristina Rodgers

Lola
Oscar Pfleeger